BEZALEL

IMAGE OF GOD

To Alison;
fear not God can
be trusted...
Chris

OTHER BOOKS BY
CHRIST JOHN OTTO

An Army Arising:
Why Artists Are on the Frontline of the Next Move of God

Body
Where You Belong
Red Book of Poetic Theology for Artists

Mary
Value and Honor
Blue Book of Poetic Theology for Artists

Drip

BEZALEL
IMAGE OF GOD

―――――

CHRIST JOHN OTTO

To Liz and Andy,
and all my friends in Kingston-upon-Hull,
my first home in the England.

Special thanks to
Courtney McDonald,
Nancy Mari,
Amanda Mandeville,
Peter Lane,
and Jörn Lange
for their invaluable help
in editing, providing feedback,
and preparing this
manuscript for publication.

CONTENTS

THE IMAGE

The Greek word, "eikon" appears in the New Testament 24 times.

Yes, it is the same word
as our modern English word, "icon."
And before the internet and emoticons,
the word icon really only meant one thing.
Icons were pictures,
and more specifically,
pictures of Jesus, Mary, and the Saints,
for use in worship and prayer.
As the Orthodox Christians like to say,
icons are designed to be windows into heaven.

The word comes from the Bible,
from this verse:

Jesus Christ is the visible image of the invisible God.
He existed before anything was created and is supreme over all creation,
for through him God created everything
   in the heavenly realms and on earth.
He made the things we can see
   and the things we can't see—
such as thrones, kingdoms, rulers, and authorities in the unseen world.
   Everything was created through him and for him.
                              (Colossians 1:15-16, NLT)

Jesus is the visible picture,
perfect portrait,
of the Invisible God.
And the passage also says
that Jesus Christ, the Image,
is also incredibly creative—
making everything we see and cannot see.
Jesus is an Icon, and a Creator.

It was this verse that ended the Iconoclast controversy of the 7th century.

You see,
long before the Protestant Reformation,
the church attempted to remove artists,
because of the influence of Islam.
They took all the artists
who were painting icons,
and they did a very Islamic thing.
They cut off their hands.

>Whenever this anti-Christ spirit rises,
>it turns to violence.
>It breaks things and people.

Yes, it was Christians
who were doing this to other Christians.
It is part of history.
Important history you need to know if you are an artist for the Kingdom.

It has always been dangerous to make the unseen visible.
There is danger in helping others see into Heaven.

And then they burned the pictures
(they were painted on wood),
and destroyed churches.
Just like during the Protestant Reformation.
This chaos ended with the Seventh Ecumenical Council,
and the restoration of the icons to the church.

Today this event is celebrated
in all Eastern Orthodox churches
on the first Sunday of Lent.

And why did they decide that images were okay in church?
Because the Bible says that Jesus is the Icon.
The Greeks saw that the New Testament called Jesus
an Icon almost 20 times.

He is the image,
and the word became Flesh,
and made the Invisible Visible,
and in seeing Jesus,
we have seen the Father.

                                        Jesus himself said this.

God sanctified
time,
space,
and humanity,
by entering in
and becoming part of it.
And we have seen him,
and we have seen his glory.
Jesus is the perfect likeness,
portrait,
and living embodiment of the Father.

Long before Jesus, the Lord needed
to create a place for his son to exist,
and a people who could provide his home.

God set out to create a little bit of heaven on earth
so his Son
would not feel completely
unwelcome
in the earth.

And the goal,
from Genesis 1:1
to Revelation 22:21,
was to find a Bride for his Son
and to give his Son a Kingdom.
The plan was to create
an outpost of heaven,
that looked like the Kingdom,
and where eating and drinking with God,
and the culture of heaven,
would begin to invade the earth.

> This is a True Story,
> in that it is the Story of Truth.
> Jesus said,
> I am the Truth.

And from the beginning,
this True Story
revealed a plan.

This book is about one of the first key people
in this True Story.
God chose
an Artist,
Artisan,
and Teacher,
to reveal the Visible Image
for the first time.

And he became
a reflection,
as in a mirror,
of that True Image,
and created
the first outpost on earth
of the Kingdom of God.

This saga is for you—
artistic,
creative,
and unconventional person,
to make the unseen visible
and prepare the way
for the King
and his Kingdom.

BEFORE THE BEGINNING

Before the beginning there was God.

Our Saga begins
before
the Bible does.
The Bible is a story, and all stories need a starting place.
The Bible story begins at Creation.

Before the beginning matters for our Tale,
and its beginning
with God creating,
and water,
and the Spirit of God.
But before the beginning there was a why.

And for you to be completely you, we need to go back before the beginning.

Before the beginning there was God.

And God
was the Most Relational Being in the Universe.

God was Father, Son, and Holy Spirit.
In relationship,
and in Love.

God is Love.
And Love demands relationship,
and Love demands a choice.
So God, the Relational Being, longed for Lovers and Friends.

So before the beginning there was a story, and a conflict.

God created angels, and mysterious beasts, and creatures.
And all of them were made to worship and serve God.
But because they were designed to glorify and serve, they could not love.

> Love demands a choice.
> We are not automatons
> pre-programmed for the glory of God.

But angels to some extent are,
and somewhere before the beginning, there was a revolt.
A "bug entered the system,"
and a third of the angels chose to worship one of their ranks.
And they fell from glory.

And after this,
God decided that he needed someone who could love him back.
And in order for this to happen, God took a risk.

He would create beings who shared most of the qualities of God,
they could choose,
they could think for themselves,
they could act on their own will,
they could conceive of new ideas,
and they could create and recreate.
They would be a little lower than God,
above the angels,
and God could relate to them,
more or less,
as equals.
These would be the Most Valuable Beings in the Universe.
God did all this, because He is the Most Relational Being in the Universe.

It was risky business.

And for this plan to work,
these new Beings needed an environment to live in.
Heaven, with its set order,
would not work.
It needed to be like a womb,
with all the resources to sustain life.
It needed to be a place that required discovery,
and taming,
and creativity,
and development.

And this good place would become home to the Little Creators.
A place where the Creator and the Little Creators
could love,
be loved,
and relate.
And also transform.

And then God made humankind,
Man and Woman he made them,
In the Image of God he created them.

And the two sexes would have to interact and relate,
because they were like God,
and God interacts and relates.
Adam was not complete alone.
Adam needed someone else,
and so did She.

And God called the Little Creators very good.

Shadows of God.
Image of God.
In Hebrew,
B'Tzelem Elohim.
Remember that.

And God said
Be fruitful and multiply,
Not just reproduction and procreation.
Be fruitful and be full in life:
create,
develop,
discover,
give names to everything you find,
and turn this wild place into a garden,
and the garden into a City that we can live in together.

Have mastery over creation and exercise dominion, just like God.

Dominion,
ruling and reigning.

                                        Not Domination,
                                          use and abuse.

Ironically, some of the very people who deny this story,
are the ones still doing that original command.
They are discovering new things,
and giving them names,
and using the things they discover,
to be fruitful.

                              No one escapes the love of God.

Behind the scenes there was still a bug in the system:
Rebellion,
deceit,
and death.

God knew,
and knows,
that to be like God there must be a choice.
Love demands it.
And built into this new venture
was the risky need to make a choice.

And the Little Creators
were presented with options,
and with the help of an Ancient Serpent,
they chose wrongly.

And the creation was subjected to futility:
to death,
domination,
slavery,
and abuse.

It was subjected to the survival of the strong,
and the destruction of the weak.
Domination by the Serpent and his allies.

It was subjected to isolation, and grief.

And God,
who made it all,
to enjoy with his Little Creators,
was no longer welcome.

And it was now a renegade creation,
run by outlaws,
hoping to
rob,
kill,
and destroy,
so the original plan would never be fulfilled.

And the Little Creators,
a little lower than God,
were told they were beasts.

And we began to act like it.

But God doesn't quit.
He didn't start over someplace else.

He loves people,
and he loves places.
And he was willing to do anything to make things right.

So God began to look for friends.
In the beginning there were not very many.
But those few were very important.
And the few became a family.
And the family became a tribe.
And the tribe became a people.
And the people,
because this was still enemy territory,
became slaves.

And this is where the real story of our book begins.

You were in the mind of the Creator before the beginning.
You were created to love, and be loved,
to be fruitful and multiply,
and there is so much work for you to do.

We are going to redeem a renegade creation,
and become Little Creators again.

CREATING A CULTURE

God uses culture to rule and reign.

And in order to create an outpost of heaven,
he needed a people to adopt the culture of heaven,
and he needed a place for that culture to operate.

God began with a friend,
and that friend was Abraham.

And God promised Abraham that his son would form a great nation.

Through many twists and turns, and a lot of family drama, his sons became
a tribe. And one day the tribe sold one of its brothers into slavery.

That brother was Joseph.

>Before we get too far,
>it will seem that I am getting off track.
>I am not.
>This story is important, because it provides context.
>And for our larger story, and the point of this book,
>context is everything.

Joseph, through even more twists and turns,
moved from slave, to prisoner, to second in command after Pharaoh!

And then he saved Egypt from famine,
and was reconciled with his family.

Abraham's family had become a people.
And the people prospered in Egypt, to the point where they became a threat.
So Egypt made them slaves, since they were foreigners in their midst.

This was all a setup.
God was about to create a nation.
A nation needs a distinct culture.
Israel the people would become Israel the nation,
with a story,
a song,
and a meal.

Story, art, and food are the building blocks of culture.

So God chose a renegade to be his agent.
Moses would become God's spokesman to Pharaoh.
And Moses would be the one who led the people to freedom.

"Let my people go," said Moses.

"No," said Pharaoh.

They had this conversation 10 times.

And with each "no" from Pharaoh, things got worse for Egypt.
10 plagues, each targeting a god in the Egyptian pantheon,
were visited upon the Egyptians.
And Egypt was devastated.
And finally, there was a final warning.

Let my people go,
or the first born of every family
and of all the livestock
would die.

And God told Moses, and the people, to do a funny thing.

Have a dinner party.

Kill a lamb,
put its blood above your door,
and eat the lamb with bitter herbs and dry unleavened bread.
And ask your neighbors for all their gold, jewelry, finery, and luxuries.

And in the midst of all the devastation in Egypt,
the Egyptians gave up their stuff,
and Israel had their dinner.

The dinner still happens, each spring,
as a reminder.
That's a powerful bit of culture.
Food and story makes us who we are.

Before morning, the first born of Egypt were dead,
and the people were on their way out of the country.

But they were still not a nation,
they were a people,
just freed from slavery.
Culture requires a change in identity.

When word reached the king of Egypt that the Israelites had fled, Pharaoh and his officials changed their minds. "What have we done, letting all those Israelite slaves get away?" they asked. So Pharaoh harnessed his chariot and called up his troops. He took with him 600 of Egypt's best chariots, along with the rest of the chariots of Egypt, each with its commander. The Lord hardened the heart of Pharaoh, the king of Egypt, so he chased after the people of Israel, who had left with fists raised in defiance. The Egyptians chased after them with all the forces in Pharaoh's army—all his horses and chariots, his charioteers, and his troops. The Egyptians caught up with the people of Israel as they were camped beside the shore near Pi-hahiroth, across from Baal-zephon.

As Pharaoh approached, the people of Israel looked up and panicked when they saw the Egyptians overtaking them. They cried out to the Lord, and they said to Moses, "Why did you bring us out here to die in the wilderness? Weren't there enough graves for us in Egypt? What have you done to us? Why did you make us leave Egypt? Didn't we tell you this would happen while we were still in Egypt? We said, 'Leave us alone! Let us be slaves to the Egyptians. It's better to be a slave in Egypt than a corpse in the wilderness!'"

But Moses told the people, "Don't be afraid. Just stand still and watch the Lord rescue you today. The Egyptians you see today will never be seen again. The Lord himself will fight for you. Just stay calm."

Then the Lord said to Moses, "Why are you crying out to me? Tell the people to get moving! Pick up your staff and raise your hand over the sea. Divide the water so the Israelites can walk through the middle of the sea on dry ground. And I will harden the hearts of the Egyptians, and they will charge in after the Israelites. My great glory will be displayed through Pharaoh and his troops, his chariots, and his charioteers. When my glory is displayed through them, all Egypt will see my glory and know that I am the Lord!"

Then the angel of God, who had been leading the people of Israel, moved to the rear of the camp. The pillar of cloud also moved from the front and stood behind them. The cloud settled between the Egyptian and Israelite camps. As darkness fell, the cloud turned to fire, lighting up the night. But the Egyptians and Israelites did not approach each other all night.

Then Moses raised his hand over the sea, and the Lord opened up a path through the water with a strong east wind. The wind blew all that night, turning the seabed into dry land. So the people of Israel walked through the middle of the sea on dry ground, with walls of water on each side!

Then the Egyptians—all of Pharaoh's horses, chariots, and charioteers—chased them into the middle of the sea. But just before dawn the Lord looked down on the Egyptian army from the pillar of fire and cloud, and he threw their forces into total confusion. He twisted their chariot wheels, making their chariots difficult to drive. "Let's get out of here—away from these Israelites!" the Egyptians shouted. "The Lord is fighting for them against Egypt!"

When all the Israelites had reached the other side, the Lord said to Moses, "Raise your hand over the sea again. Then the waters will rush back and cover the Egyptians and their chariots and charioteers." So as the sun began to rise, Moses raised his hand over the sea, and the water rushed back into its usual place. The Egyptians tried to escape, but the Lord swept them into the sea. Then the waters returned and covered all the chariots and charioteers—the entire army of Pharaoh. Of all the Egyptians who had chased the Israelites into the sea, not a single one survived.

But the people of Israel had walked through the middle of the sea on dry ground, as the water stood up like a wall on both sides. That is how the Lord rescued Israel from the hand of the Egyptians that day. And the Israelites saw the bodies of the Egyptians washed up on the seashore. When the people of Israel saw the mighty power that the Lord had unleashed against the Egyptians, they were filled with awe before him. They put their faith in the Lord and in his servant Moses.

Then Moses and the people of Israel sang this song to the Lord:

"I will sing to the Lord,
  for he has triumphed gloriously;
  he has hurled both horse and rider
  into the sea.
The Lord is my strength and my song;
  he has given me victory. (Exodus 14:5-15:2, NLT)

In one night a people
in a baptism
through the sea,
had become a nation.

On the other side of the sea they had the building blocks of culture.
A story,
a song,
and a meal.

God uses culture to rule and reign on the earth.
Artists and creative people are essential.
You are the ones who communicate, preserve, and build a culture.
Art, food, and story make us who we are.

After the sea, God had more to say to Moses,
and the people went to a mountain,
and God met with Moses.

It was all about culture again.
God gave Moses a moral code that set them apart from the other nations.
He gave them holidays.
He set the calendar,
and gave them rest.
Rest is a big deal after being a slave.

And then God told them they would be given land
at the crossroads of humanity,
on an ancient trade route,
and said they would live their unique way
where everyone could see.

Remember, this was always about creating a place on the earth
for man and God to have relationship.
It was about taking territory,
and making holy space in the earth.

And Moses came down from the mountain and a funny thing happened.

There are a lot of funny things in this story,
none of it is what you expect.

                                    God throws a dinner party.
But before they do, there is a bloodbath.
Moses sacrifices a bull and dashes the blood against the altar,
the book of the covenant, and the people.

And then, covered with blood,
Moses and the elders of Israel go and meet God on the mountain.
And they walk upon a clear sapphire pavement,
and they see God face to face, and
they eat and drink together.

You see, they have encountered the Most Relational Being in the Universe.
Not the "angry God of the Old Testament." The whole point of this story
is to eat and drink with God in an outpost of heaven.

And the elders leave Moses, and Moses stays on the mountain with God
and learns the plans for the future.

Israel is about to have a physical model of heavenly things,
of mysteries yet to be fulfilled,
And it is going to be filled with glorious color,
made from the former riches of Egypt.
And this place will be a place where God and man can eat together in
Fellowship.

And this place will be portable,
And all the nations who interact with Israel will see
their portable outpost of heaven.

But Moses was no artist or artisan.
He did not have the skills to make such a place.
And so, in the midst of the time on the mountain,
God mentions two other men by name, apart from Aaron.
God reveals to Moses
that people
are always the greatest resource
in his Kingdom,
and he names Bezalel.

and his assistant Oholiab.

The only people called by God, other than Aaron, are artists.

> Then the Lord said to Moses, "Look, I have specifically chosen Bezalel son of Uri, grandson of Hur, of the tribe of Judah. I have filled him with the Spirit of God, giving him great wisdom, ability, and expertise in all kinds of crafts. He is a master craftsman, expert in working with gold, silver, and bronze. He is skilled in engraving and mounting gemstones and in carving wood. He is a master at every craft!
>
> "And I have personally appointed Oholiab son of Ahisamach, of the tribe of Dan, to be his assistant. Moreover, I have given special skill to all the gifted craftsmen so they can make all the things I have commanded you to make:
>
> the Tabernacle;
> the Ark of the Covenant;
> the Ark's cover—the place of atonement;
> all the furnishings of the Tabernacle;
> the table and its utensils;
> the pure gold lampstand with all its accessories;
> the incense altar;
> the altar of burnt offering with all its utensils;
> the washbasin with its stand;
> the beautifully stitched garments—the sacred garments for Aaron the priest, and the garments for his sons to wear as they minister as priests;
> the anointing oil;
> the fragrant incense for the Holy Place.
> The craftsmen must make everything as I have commanded you."
>   (Exodus 31:1-11, NLT)

IDENTITY IS EVERYTHING

Reading and studying the Bible can be like playing six dimensional chess.
The Hebrew language is multi-dimensional.

Hebrew letters are really pictures,
and they can be rearranged
and put back together and still say the same thing.
And sometimes there are roots
that connect words that to us seem disconnected.

For instance,
"sacrifice" shares the same root as "family."

You could ponder that one all day.

In Hebrew "sacrifice" means to come close.

And the same thing happens with names.

When someone gets a name in the Bible,
that name is not just a label.
That name is a descriptor of the person.

It tells us who that person is,
what their purpose is,
and identifies them at a deep level.

Identity is everything.

And if you look at a person's name
and you look at the expression of their life,
the name and the life will go together.

And sometimes the name precedes the purpose.
And sometimes the name becomes the person.
And sometimes the person becomes the name.

This is why, so often, a person gets a new name when they have an encounter
with God.

So Abram,
which means "exalted father"
became Abraham,
"Father of Many Nations."

Jacob,
Heel-Grabber,
becomes Israel,
The One Who Contends with God.

Simon,
the Listener,
becomes Peter,
the Rock.

And many Biblical names have layers.
The first layer is obvious,
but the more you dig,
the more you find.

Bezalel is one of those names.

If you open any Biblical dictionary,
they will tell you that Bezalel means
"the shadow of God."

And as a person who has taught on this many times,
smug people with a Bible app will look at you and say they know it all,
when they really know almost nothing.

Yes, Bezalel means, "Shadow of God."
But not in the sense of dwelling in the shade of protection,
like in Psalm 91:
"dwelling in the shadow of the Almighty."

No in this case,
shadow is like a reflection.
Like the shape of the original cast upon the ground.
Like Plato's shadows on the back of the cave
that reflect the True.
Or as we say in English,
"a chip off the old block"
or the "apple doesn't fall far from the tree."

Bezalel is a small copy of the original.

                                        But wait,
                                  there's more.

At the time of the New Testament,
philosophers and scholars
believed that God was the original "Sound."
They suggested that over time
God was sending out echoes of himself,
and like an echo,
each one was slightly weaker than the previous one.
And the name they gave each of these echoes
was "Logos."

John, began his gospel with
"In the beginning was the Logos."
And says Jesus is the Logos.

                        Rather than an echo, Jesus is the original Sound.

Well Philo, a Jewish philosopher around that time,
said a similar thing.

Bezalel, so he thought, was a "Logos"
an emanation from the divine,
an expression of God.
An echo of the original.

And then there is more.

Remember when I told you about the beginning,
and the two first members of humankind,
Adam and Eve?
And what God said about them?
In the Image of God He created them.
In Hebrew:
B'Tzelem Elohim.
(That's pronounced BETZ-ellem el-OH-eem)

Bezalel.
(That's pronounced BETZ-ah-lel)

Any similarities?

Hebrew letters have their origins in ancient word pictures.
Each word is made of a root,
the core idea and picture of a word.
And words are formed off the roots.
Letters can be moved around or removed
and the pictures remain the same.

If you look at the roots and the letters in Hebrew,
the name Bezalel retains the roots of Genesis 1:26.
The word picture remains the same,
and when you say it out loud,
You can hear the name in the phrase.
The picture is "the image of God."

Bezalel is the Image of God.

And the Image of God given to us is
an artist,
an artisan,
a master craftsman,
called to create a place for God in the earth.

And everything from here on
in this book is about being an artist in the image of God.

And all the qualities and gifts and graces Bezalel received
define
and describe
what it means to be a Little Creator,
the image of God.

You have probably been named wrongly,
defined,
labeled
or described badly.

That's why I don't use the term
"creatives"
to describe my tribe.
"Creatives" is just another label.

Labels limit,
and labels are shorthand,
to keep you from getting to know someone
and honor them for who they are.

Because you are a Little Creator,
and just like the Big One,
there is an aspect to you
that is eternal,
and infinite.
You were created to endlessly become.

You might be living under the cloud of the names and labels some person put on you.

Today I want to tell you
that you can be free.

But first you have to forgive them.

You have to say,
"Person, I forgive you for calling me that name."

And you have to say to yourself,
"Me, I forgive you for taking on that name,
  and agreeing with it,
  and allowing it to stunt your growth,
  and your endless becoming."

And you have to ask Jesus to wash you,
  and cleanse you,
  and you have to renounce those names,
  and receive the real one that God has given you.

Lord, we receive the name that you give us,
  and every good and perfect gift that comes from being
  made in your Image.

BELONGING

Identity is everything,
and so is belonging.

And so, when God called Bezalel,
and named him before Moses,
God gave us his name and address,
so to speak.

God calls Bezalel by name,
but also by his family,
and by his tribe.

I think some of this is so Moses could find him in the crowds.

But also,
because place is very important.

Bezalel belongs to a family,
and to a tribe.

A tribe is a family of families.
It's a sub-culture.
A group with unique values and identities.

Bezalel's grandfather, Hur,
must have been close to Moses,
and he was.
He was Moses' brother in law.

And he was also the father of Caleb--
Caleb was the one who had faith along with Joshua to go into the promised
land.

Bezalel comes from a family of faith and leadership.

Those are unique qualities and values.

And he comes from a tribe,
the Tribe of Judah.

From the beginning,
Judah was different.

He was willing to self-sacrifice for the life of
Benjamin in the story of Joseph.

And at the end of Genesis,
when Israel blesses his sons,
this is what he says over Judah:

> The scepter will not depart from Judah,
>   nor the ruler's staff from his descendants,
> until the coming of the one to whom it belongs,
>   the one whom all nations will honor.
> He ties his foal to a grapevine,
>   the colt of his donkey to a choice vine.
> He washes his clothes in wine,
>   his robes in the blood of grapes.
> His eyes are darker than wine,
>   and his teeth are whiter than milk. (Genesis 49:10-12, NLT)

This is a promise,
a promise about the Messiah.
It foretells Jesus riding into Jerusalem
and shedding his own blood.

And there is a promise about a kingdom.
This tribe is destined for Royalty.

And this tribe would produce David,
and Solomon,
and Joseph,
and Mary,
and Jesus.

A tribe and its culture help you know where you belong,
and this tribe is where Bezalel lived.

A long time ago now,
I remember a man named Leonard Sweet
ranting in a seminary.

(If you read my other books,
please forgive me,
I have said this before.)

And he said,
the church of the future is
tribal,
global,
and post-denominational.

I think what he meant was,
the future was not about labels
but about values.

And the things you value,
will determine your friends
and associates.

It will not be about the sign above the door,
but about the way you see the world,
and about the way you do things.

My marketing guru Seth Godin describes a tribe this way:
"People like us do things like this."

So Bezalel,
the artist in the Image of God,
the Little Creator,
was also
the genetic material of kings,
and an ancestor of the Messiah.

Bezalel,
the artist in the Image of God,
the Little Creator,
was also from a people
who held self-sacrifice,
faith in God,
and belief in his promises,
as a core value.

I guess it's no surprise that God called this one to build an outpost of heaven.

In fact,
it sounds like he was created
before time began
to do this.

One day a funny thing happened to me in Boston,
I went to the Gay Pride Parade.
This wasn't my plan,
as so often happens,
I got off my stated plan,
and God diverted me so I could learn something.

There were a lot of people at the Gay Pride parade.
And it soon became clear to me
that most of the folks at the parade
were not gay.

Hmm.
I had a revelation.
The gay community is a very defined tribe,
and it has a lot of sub-tribes.
And these tribes have different defining attributes.

This is a family book,
so I will leave it there.

The average Joe and Jane Schmo
from the suburbs,
attending Boston University,
are from a world where there are no tribes,
and they have an identity crisis.

They are not sure who they are
because they are not sure where they belong.
And Boston University, and the public schools,
and the media,
have told them that they are "nothings,"
who have evolved from nothing,
for no apparent reason.
And their only value comes from
being the fittest,
the richest,
the sexiest,
and the most successful
to survive.

And so,
putting on a rainbow,
going to a raucous party,
and feeling like a member of a tribe for a day,
makes a lot of sense.

Christians think it is about morality
and they lament.
It's not.

It's about belonging.

Meanwhile the church thinks
if you make yourself
less distinct from the
tribe-less culture,
and lower the bar for membership—

You, know,
no distinction between who is in
and who is out,
—you will gain.

You lose.
And people become more confused,
and less sure of who they are.
They think they are welcoming the stranger,
by letting unbelievers take communion,
not requiring life change,
or change in attitudes.
They are just saying that what they believe,
and who they are is a nothing.
The brand has lost its meaning.

> If you take down the door,
> there is no longer a house.
> And no one feels safe anymore.
> Dietrich Bonheoffer called this "cheap grace."

But Jesus,
created a tribe,
and it is an extension of the one that Bezalel came from.
The one that believes

self-sacrifice,
faith in God,
and belief in promises,
are core values.

A holy priesthood,
a called out nation,
a peculiar people,
chosen.

And there are insiders and outsiders.
Everybody is invited,
but not everybody attends.

The whole world is in transition right now,
as the church goes through a re-formation.

There is nothing wrong
with you finding the people who share your values,
and who do things the way you do.
People might tell you that's wrong,
but it's not.

You need a place
and a people
to belong to.

Hopefully,
those are Kingdom people,
who value you,
and not just what you can do for them.

A tribe makes you who you are,
and supports your true identity.

And once you know where you belong,
you can flourish,
and belonging creates an environment

that makes you fruitful.
Jesus,
may I be in you as You are in the Father,
and may that place of belonging in You
lead me to the people who
will be my tribe.
May I flourish
in the safety,
of a family
and a people
who love me.

BEZALEL WAS FILLED

I have been studying Bezalel for about 10 years.
That is about the time it takes to do a Ph.D.

Three of those years Bezalel was my primary focus,
along with loving,
encouraging,
and making disciples
of artists and creative people.

One day,
while doing research at
Gordon-Conwell Theological Seminary
I discovered something strange.

No one had written a book about Bezalel.
Nor had anyone done a doctoral dissertation.
Or an extensive commentary on him.

There are reasons for this,
and I will address them later.

But I mention it
because Bezalel is a profound person,
and completely unique,
as so many artistic people are.

So what makes him so special,
and what sets him apart?

He was filled with the Spirit of God.

No other person in the Old Covenant experienced this.

And it is important.
Because of the Reformation and Enlightenment,
many in the church made war on the artist.
And this is one of the reasons Bezalel was overlooked and neglected.

It's a crime.

It also highlights
a fundamental mistake
that some people make
about Christianity and the New Covenant.

The New Covenant is about the Holy Spirit.

The Holy Spirit
was promised
by the Prophets,
and Promised by Jesus.
And it wasn't until after the Resurrection
that the church was born,
after the descent of the Holy Spirit.
The Holy Spirit created the Church.

The New Covenant is about the Holy Spirit.
Just read the Fathers from the first few centuries of the Church.

And yet, here is a man,
in the Old Covenant,
and it says that he was filled with the Spirit of God.

Every other time the Holy Spirit is mentioned in the Hebrew Scriptures,
the Spirit comes "upon" the person,
for a specific purpose,
or a specific task.

David mentions this in Psalm 51 when he begs God
to not take the Holy Spirit away.

All the prophets,
David,
King Saul,
and Samson,
had an experience of the Spirit coming upon them.
Usually to accomplish a task,
and when the task was finished,
the Spirit lifted.

That is outside in,
not inside out.

But Bezalel was filled.
That is inside out.

Now you may say this is just semantics,
or you may raise arguments.
But what happened to Bezalel is unique.

As I mentioned earlier,
Hebrew is a fascinating language.

In English, we have basically three kinds of verb tenses:
past, present, and future.
There are variations on these three,
but essentially we think of actions as
in the past,
in the present,
or in the future.

Hebrew thinks of actions as
past,
future, continuous,
moving through dimensions,
and present.
They have tenses that indicate movement.
And
they have tenses that indicate time and eternity.

And here in Exodus 31,
the Hebrew phrase "Filled with the Spirit of God,"
is one of these unusual verb tenses.

We can't actually translate this one word into English accurately.
We have to describe it.
It would go something like this:

"I have begun filling Bezalel with the Spirit of God,
and that filling will be continuous,
and ongoing
and never ending
and the flow will spill out onto others,
and infuse all that he touches."

It is no surprise that immediately
God lists the seventeen gifts he received as a result.

Jesus said something like this in John's Gospel:
Out of your belly will flow rivers of living water.

Whoosh.
That's being filled.
And that's the New Covenant.

I have attended many boring parties
with Christian college art professors.
Inevitably, the conversation drifts to two tired topics:

38

"What is Christian art?"

(or its boring variation,
"Is there such a thing as Christian art?")

and

"Why is Christian art so bad?"

Yawn.

And of course, it always ends up in a conundrum.
There are no answers when you talk
out of post-modern philosophical grids,
where everything is relative,
on a continuum of
the world, the flesh, and the devil,
that doesn't allow
absolutes
or value judgements,
and won't admit ugly is ugly,
or pagan is pagan.
It's not all good.

Bezalel shows us a better way,
the way of the Kingdom.

Bezalel was called to create something
that would break into a fallen, rebellious creation,
and become a signpost to heaven.
Bezalel was filled
to create a three dimensional prophecy
of the coming of God's Kingdom in Jesus Christ.
He did this without a roadmap,
or an encounter on the mountain.

Stephen,
before he became the first martyr,
enraged his accusers,
because he did what Jesus said to do:

"Wait and let the Holy Spirit speak for you and give an account."
The Holy Spirit gave him words to say,
and no one could argue with him.

And Bezalel, in the same way,
from the inside out,
would be guided by the Holy Spirit,
and that inner guidance would be the
plan,
initiation,
education,
and
direction for his work.
Artists in the Kingdom
are meant to be Little Creators,
and the only way to do that,
and not be just like everybody else,
is to be filled with the Holy Spirit.

The One who hovered over the waters at Creation,
wants to fill you with the same Waters of Life
that make glad the City of God,
and give life to everything you touch.
And out of your belly will flow rivers
that inspire,
transform,
illuminate,
and revive.

The Source of your creative ability
will make you different,
if you want to be the kind of person that Bezalel was.
The same power,
anointing,
and ability
is available to you.

Throughout history,
every person who was ever given the title
"Miracle Worker"
would pray this prayer every day.
And this is a great prayer to pray
if you want to create something for God,
and something that will change the world.

Come, Holy Spirit,
send forth the heavenly
radiance of your light.

Come, Father of the poor,
come giver of gifts,
come, light of the heart.

Greatest Comforter,
sweet guest of the soul,
sweet consolation.

In labor, rest,
in heat, temperance,
in tears, solace.

O most blessed Light,
fill the inmost heart
of your faithful.

Without your divine will,
there is nothing in man,
nothing is harmless.

Wash that which is unclean,
water that which is dry,
heal that which is wounded.

Bend that which is inflexible,
warm that which is chilled,
make right that which is wrong.

Give to your faithful,
who rely on you,
the sevenfold gifts.

Give reward to virtue,
give salvation at our passing on,
give eternal joy.
Amen. Alleluia.

SEVENTEEN

As an artist,
I find symbolic language fascinating.
Life is made of little things,
and all of them are symbols.

Since the Enlightenment,
there has been a full scale war on symbols.
And many people do not understand the language
and messages happening all around us.
This is ironic, since we probably live
in the most symbolic age in history.

Hebrew is one of the most symbolic languages.
It often says more than words.
I am very interested in what Hebrew
is saying without saying a word.
Patterns,
numbers,
and pictures
are written deep into the text.

In the last chapter
I talked about how Bezalel was filled.
And the text says:

"I have filled him with the Spirit of God, and with
   ability,
   intelligence,
   and knowledge of every kind of craft.
   to devise artistic designs,
   to work in gold, silver, and bronze.
   in cutting stones for setting,
   and in carving wood,
   in every kind of craft.
   And I have inspired him to teach,
   I have filled them with skill
   to do every kind of work
   done by an artisan or designer,
   or by an embroiderer,
   in blue, purple, or crimson yarns,
   or by a weaver,
   or work by any sort of artisan
   or skilled designer." (Exodus 35:30-35, NLT)

This list is from the second call of Bezalel in Exodus 35.

It's a comprehensive list of all the skills
needed to create this multisensory
traveling
worship tent.

And the skills are described in groups.
It begins with intellectual and administrative ability.
And among that first group is a word in Hebrew
that should be translated
"business sense."

The Holy Spirit
gave Bezalel
a head for business.
He gave him the ability to manage money wisely,
make shrewd business decisions,
and make the most of every opportunity.

There is nothing wrong with you making money,
and prospering from the work of your hands.
God wants to bless you to be a blessing for others.
That's why you have gifts.

You might want to stop right now and ask for that gift yourself.

The Holy Spirit gave Bezalel
comprehensive knowledge,
in every kind of craft.
I hope he wasn't annoying at parties,
because knowing about everything can be annoying.
But knowledge is essential if you want to be a leader,
to have a grasp of the process
and the procedure
of every aspect of the project.

Then the Holy Spirit gives him
the gifts of sculpture and metalwork.
Yes, the first skill he receives is the ability
to make statues.
He is going to make
cherubim,
pomegranates,
almond branches,
and many other beautiful things.
And I am guessing,
when Moses needed the bronze serpent,
he probably called the guy who knew how to work in bronze,
to make it.

God gave him the ability to work in jewels
to etch names on them, to be exact
so he could make Aaron's breastplate.
He was able to carve wood.

And most important of all:
He was given the ability to teach.

He had the supernatural gift to impart to others
all the skills he had received,
so that the knowledge and ability
didn't die with him.
This is a living thing.
God is creating a culture of creativity,
and birthing a symbolic system
to represent his kingdom on earth.

When I was studying this the first time,
I counted the words in the Hebrew.
I came up with seventeen.

I thought, "Hmmm,
that's unusual."

Seventeen is an unusual number,
a prime number,
and not one you come across in life
or the Bible very often.

I shared this with my friend Randall Worley
and he got very excited.

Here's why.

The Passover happened on the 14th day of the month.
Exodus makes note of this date several times.
It will take them two days to reach the Red Sea.
And it says that there was a strong east wind all night,
and they crossed through the sea on dry ground.
And then,
the Egyptians
followed them into the sea,
and they drowned.

And then,
thousands of years later,

Jesus died on the cross,
on the 14th day of the same month,
and three days later,
he stepped out of the tomb.

Both these events happened on the seventeenth day of the month.

Seventeen is the number of complete and total victory.

God's victory over Egypt,
and over the Serpent,
was displayed when he gave Bezalel
the gifts to build the first
outpost of heaven on the earth.

Through his creative gifts,
and the indwelling Holy Spirit,
God accomplished the first D-Day invasion
of his kingdom.

You may think that Bezalel the artist wasn't a big deal.
You may think that the Tabernacle was a nice thing.

This is the establishing of true worship on the earth
for the first time since the fall,
and making a place where God and humanity
could be close again.

The call and anointing of Bezalel
was one of the most cataclysmic events in history.

You may think
that the gifts you have been given
are for yourself.

Maybe you think that your abilities
are fine as hobbies.
Maybe you think that what you do is not important.

Every good and perfect gift
has been given to you by your Father
to be a sign and an outpost of heaven.
You have no idea the difference
one song,
one picture,
one story,
one film,
one video game,
and on, and on,
can make in the world.

There are those who need to receive
a revelation from heaven.
And the only ones who can
give that revelation
are the ones who are connected to the King of Heaven.

Your gifts and abilities
are the signs and weapons
of God's overwhelming,
complete and total
victory,
in reclaiming
planet earth.

Your art
is a weapon
of truth,
goodness,
justice,
righteousness,
sanctity,
purity,
life,
and
freedom.

You need the ability
to manage those gifts,
and impart them to others.
And that ability
comes from the Holy Spirit.

O Lord,
may we receive the seventeen-fold indwelling
presence of your Spirit,
to fill us with sense and ability,
skill and insight.
May we be able to pursue excellence with ease,
and reveal the unseen to those who need to see.
May we teach and impart to others
and be generous with our gifts.
May our creative output create
a mighty kingdom revolution
releasing your will on the earth.
Amen.

AARON MADE A CALF

Before we get to the best part of the story
we have to walk through a dark chapter.

Moses lingered on the mountain.
I know he must have been enjoying his time with God. After God told him
about Bezalel, he told him about Sabbath. And then God gave him the first
tablets that recorded their conversation.

Meanwhile,
down below,
there was murmuring.

Following a call from God is going to set you apart,
and rarely do those you leave behind understand.

Moses was gone for more than a month.
There were several million people, recently freed from slavery, camped out
in the desert. Eventually there would be problems, and someone had to
keep order.

Some called for a god, and for a pagan style festival. They had been told
when they left Egypt they were going out into the desert to have a festival
to the Lord.

Where's the festival?

Sometimes God takes you out into a secluded place, and he makes you wait for the promise. And in the waiting, you discover what's really inside. The desert lays bare your heart.

And several things become clear.

Aaron is a typical middle manager.
He didn't have the encounters with God. And if you notice, in Exodus, Aaron starts out as Moses' mouthpiece, but eventually, as Moses becomes confident, Aaron is "made redundant." No one needs his services anymore.

And when Moses went up the mountain,
no one is left in charge.
It falls upon Aaron to keep the peace--
with no revelation,
no sense of purpose or direction,
and no direct link to God.

And Aaron does what politicians and middle managers always do.

He succumbs to a small but vocal minority and gives them what they want: pagan worship.

There are three things that always get "sugar coated" in this story.
I am assuming you know it,
but if you don't,
go read Exodus 32.
I personally feel this story has gotten too much attention,
so I am not going to retell it.

The three overlooked things are:

First,
the golden calf was made in a mold. It was cast, so that like all pagan idols, it could be reproduced and sold. The idol worship of the ancient world always had a merchandising aspect to it.

Artists often get told that making art is idolatry.
No, in Exodus, making cast objects in a mold and calling them gods is
idolatry. We will talk about this later.

Second,
A very small minority of Israel actually called for and participated in the
worship of the golden calf. It says they killed three thousand out of an
estimated three million people.

Third,
Aaron acted as the leader,
made the decision,
made the calf,
and led the worship.

Lots of books and writers ignore this.
Actually, I think this might be the first place where I have seen it in print.
And somehow,
Aaron,
the idolater in chief,
was spared.
Idolatry breeds injustice.

And one final point that I think is often overlooked.
When Moses came down from the mountain,
after interceding for the people,
and saving their lives,
he was pretty angry.

And in his rage,
Moses doesn't punch out his brother Aaron,
or take a club to the golden calf.

He breaks the most precious thing ever made,
a pair of tablets,
carved by God,
inscribed with his own hand.

The Bible only records one other time God used his finger to write.
And that other time saved a woman's life.

This time,
the writing was lost in a fit of rage,
and three thousand people died.

When you start breaking things,
believing you are a self appointed reformer,
and purging impurity,
you never know when to stop.
And you end up destroying
the precious along with the profane.

One day I was using a Bible app on my phone
when a little message popped up.

They were promoting a series of five minute videos that presented an
overview of the Bible. The new video was on Exodus.

And boldly, the video stated that Exodus ends with the story of the golden
calf, because the point of Exodus is that we are not to make images and
worship them.

I was angry,
because it was a lie.
A lie that gets repeated often.

For the record,
Exodus is about how God made a new nation by freeing them from slavery,
with a mighty hand
and an outstretched arm,
and then established them as a worshipping people
around a replica of heaven.

Exodus continues for 8 more chapters after the golden calf.
And those chapters are about
making art for the true worship of God.

Exodus ends with true worship, not idolatry.
But this golden calf story looms large,
and comes up again and again when you work with Christians in the arts.
When I wrote my book *An Army Arising*,
I committed to not beginning my book
in the traditional way books for Christians in the arts began,
with an apology and a defense of the arts.
It was time to start from a new place.

John Calvin was the first to tell this falsehood about idolatry in Exodus,
he was influenced by Andreas Carlstadt and Huldrych Zwingli.
Yes, I'm naming names.

Calvin was a lawyer and a professor.
Calvin did not become a reformer after serving in the church,
or being a priest or pastor.
And I think this is very important to remember.
He was not a shepherd.
He was a wiz at convincing others of "his truth."
This is what lawyers do.
He was also the founder of a movement,
and so even little decisions he made
would infect the DNA of everything that followed.

Founding movements is like conceiving a baby.
The things that happen at the beginning
impact all the later development.

Calvin in his commentaries did something that was deliberate.
He "harmonized" the 5 books of Moses.
He did the same thing to the Gospels
rather
than write commentaries on each book.

At first this seems logical,
until you give a closer look.
And then you find that Calvin eliminated
anything he did not like.

Today we would call this "airbrushing."

And oddly,
those who follow him,
have no curiosity about the sections that are missing.
And if you do research,
you find Calvin's original statements
repeated hundreds of times,
by hundreds of commentators.
Passed on, from teacher to pupil,
for hundreds of years.
And that is why,
Protestants become obsessed with idols and idolatry,
and why they continually tear down things they misunderstand,
or they disagree with,
and why there have been no books on Bezalel.

And why Christian artists quietly accept the lie
that the Bible gives them no role model
and precedent,
when in truth, the Bible identifies an artist,
and speaks about him in the highest terms.

Bezalel was given more space in the Bible
than Noah,
Gideon,
Samson,
Ruth,
and
Elijah.

And Calvin wasn't interested.

Many people accept that we now live in a multi-sensory world,
where the arts and creative industries play an important role.
These same people believe we need to reach the culture,
and the arts are essential.
They know that the house must be built by creative people.

But one cannot build a house that says artists are necessary,
and simultaneously believe that artists are idolators,
and their work is suspect.

That's crazy-making.
And I deal with this in the church all the time.
The philosophical foundation is shaky.
And sadly, when I bring this up with leaders,
the response tends to be:
"You are thinking too much."

In the first book of Samuel,
Saul was told that rebellion is as the sin of witchcraft,
and stubbornness is equal to idolatry.
That second part doesn't get quoted very often.

The late Derek Prince once said that
"stubbornness is making an idol of your own opinion."

Sometimes we have to acknowledge the "elephant in the room."
Sometimes we have to acknowledge
that the reformation of the church
as Wesley said
must always continue.
The protestant reformers
who were zealous for the destruction of idols
built many idols themselves.

Calvin himself believed the human heart was a "factory for idols,"
and his comment was probably a rare moment of self-revelation.
Calvin's zeal for cleansing the church
hurt many people,
and several cultures.

I live in Britain,
where many monasteries and churches
were destroyed or altered during the Reformation.

I often look at the missing windows
in medieval churches
or the empty niches where sculptures once stood.
I wonder,
and long to see what was once there.
Just like I long to see those missing tablets
Moses smashed on the ground.

I want to know the handwriting of God,
but it is gone.

In the Renaissance
Scotland had one of the largest schools of composers in Europe.
The Scots are a singing people.
Today all the manuscripts are gone,
because John Knox had them burned.
And he forbade singing in church.
I wonder what those songs were like,
and how they could have changed the soul of Scotland.

Today Scotland, for the most part,
has rejected Christianity.

I think of the women
hung on the gallows in Boston,
because they believed God was speaking to them,
and had Bible studies in their homes.
In 1804 Harvard University officially rejected the divinity of Christ.

Greater Boston is considered the first "Post-Christian"
region in the United States.

I think of the pastor who lost his wife to cancer,
and he could not reconcile suffering
with predestination and sovereignty.
He just could not accept that his wife "suffered for the glory of God."
So he gave up his faith but kept on preaching.

Our churches are full of folks getting a pension
while preaching a form of godliness with no power.

I think of the young thinking Christians,
who have been told that reformed thought is evangelical theology,
and the truth is the monopoly of a "gospel coalition,"
and that in order to be loving
they have to reject orthodox faith
and the authority of the Bible,
when Wesley
and the Fathers
were compassionate and
changed the two greatest empires in history
without a whiff of Calvinism.

And every artist I have mentored and counseled
who gave up their art for a "real job,"
 or to become missionaries and then crashed and burned,
or left church because there was no place for the artist,
who embraced drugs, sex, and Buddhism
because the church had morality but no vitality,
and someone told them their wild imaginations were vain.

All these folks are scarred,
because Calvin left chapters out of his Bible.
And all the seeds of his beliefs
bore the fruit of unexpected consequences.

You are probably reading this book
because you make things,
dream dreams,
or express yourself in unconventional ways.
This was by design.
There is a place in every human heart
that is reaching for God,
and longing to make the unseen
visible.

I'm sorry for every leader who ever hurt you,
who was given permission to be an Aaron,
making idols of one man's opinions.
And bowing down to intellect over imagination.
The answers the reformers gave us
were to questions no one is asking today.

You have permission to lay aside those unquestioned answers,
and listen to the questions
people are asking today.

Who am I?
Do I have value?
Where do I belong?

Today I give you permission
to not make graven images,
plastic mass produced idols from the Oriental Trading Company,
made in Asian sweat shops but stamped with "Jesus Loves You."
Sad copies of original ideas,
retro-fitted to sell in Bible Bookstores.

Today I give you permission
to have your own
face to face
encounter
with the Author of Beauty,
and read the Bible passages
that nobody was curious enough to read.

All of creation is groaning
for thinking worshippers,
whose great minds are filled with the Holy Spirit.
Give me an army of anointed,
intelligent,
creative people,
and we will change this world in less than a generation.

Oh for a flood on the thirsty land,
Oh for a mighty revival.
Oh for a sanctified, fearless band,
ready to hail its arrival!

There is always more,
and there is endless becoming,
growing,
learning,
and Being.

For all people who were ignorant of God
were foolish by nature;
and they were unable
from the good things that are seen
to know the one who exists,
nor did they recognize the Artisan
while paying heed to his works;
but they supposed that either fire or wind or swift air,
or the circle of the stars, or turbulent water,
or the luminaries of heaven
were the gods that rule the world.

If through delight in the beauty of these things
people assumed them to be gods,
let them know how much better than these is their Lord,
for the Author of Beauty created them.

And if people were amazed at their power and working,
let them perceive from them
how much more powerful
is the one who formed them.
For from the greatness and beauty of created things
comes a corresponding perception of their Creator.

Yet these people are little to be blamed,
for perhaps they go astray
while seeking God and desiring to find him.

For while they live among his works,
they keep searching,
and they trust in what they see,
because the things that are seen are beautiful.

(Wisdom of Solomon 13:1-7)

FROM THE HEART

Following the golden calf episode
Moses returned to the mountain,
and he received a second set of tablets.
And all the goodness of the Lord passed before him,
and the Lord said a few things.

Remember the plan?
Retaking a renegade creation,
Israel being a sign about the goodness of God?
Remember creating a place for God and humankind to live in love?

It's all there in Exodus 34.

God says,
"I hereby make a covenant."

God, not Israel, makes the covenant.
God is usually the Initiator,
and we respond.

"Before all your people I will perform marvels,
such has not been performed in the earth or in any nation;
and all the people among whom you live
shall see the work of the Lord,
For it is an awesome thing that I shall do with you." (Exodus 34:10)

God makes a covenant to do awesome things
for all the other nations to see.

That piece of land in the Middle East
is a crossroads.
And these folks are there so the whole world,
every trader and traveler,
would see how good this God is.

Remember, there is a plan.

And then the Lord talks to Moses about idolatry.
And he makes two clear statements:

You shall not make cast idols. (Exodus 34:17)

You shall not appear before Me empty handed. (Exodus 34:20b)

Worship, art, and territory are all interconnected.

The making of images in Exodus is never forbidden.
The worship of other gods is forbidden,
and this worship is expressed in making idols.

This is very important,
and will be important later.
Because God commands Bezalel to make images.

Mass produced,
cast in a foundry,
and copied
was forbidden.

The God of Israel demands original worship.
The God of the Bible loves the "one of a kind,"
and God loves the products of imagination.
He commands hand hammered images.

One of a kind,
never to be copied
images.

The two cherubim
were not identical.

And Moses,
after encountering the goodness of God,
shines with his glory.
And he calls the people
and renews the covenant.

And then Moses tells them
about the place for God in the earth.
A tent to meet with God,
to eat and drink with God,
in a replica of heaven,
that will be carried throughout the land.

This place would be seen by other nations,
and they would see
how awesome
and how good this God was.

After all this,
with a shining face,
Moses calls the people together.

And rather than a tax
or a tribute,
Moses extends an invitation to
everyone who has a generous heart.

And everyone whose heart was stirred.
And everyone of a willing heart.
And everyone whose heart moved them, and were able.

And Moses reminded them of all the riches
they received as they left Egypt.

Gold, silver, and bronze;
blue, purple, and scarlet thread;
fine linen and goat hair for cloth;
tanned ram skins and fine goatskin leather;
acacia wood;
olive oil for the lamps;
spices for the anointing oil and the fragrant incense;
onyx stones, and other gemstones to be set in the ephod
and the priest's breastplate. (Exodus 35:5-9, NLT)
And he also made a second call,
not for things,
but for people.

Israel had labored
in one of the greatest empires in history.
They had learned many things.
Moses invited the skillful to come.

Our greatest resource
is always people.
People matter to God.
And people matter in this offering.

Skills and ingenuity
are far more valuable
than money or resources.
Because the skilful can do the most with the least,
and can steward resources wisely.

Again,
this is about worship.
It's about the inside out,
not the outside in.

This was a move of the Holy Spirit,
stirring the people,
and motivating the people to give
of the riches they had received.
And also moving them to offer
themselves,
in the building of a place for God.

So the whole community of Israel left Moses
and returned to their tents.
All whose hearts were stirred
and whose spirits were moved
came and brought their sacred offerings to the Lord.

> They brought all the materials needed for the Tabernacle,
> for the performance of its rituals,
> and for the sacred garments.
> Both men and women came,
> all whose hearts were willing.

> They brought to the Lord their offerings of gold—brooches,
> earrings, rings from their fingers, and necklaces. They presented
> gold objects of every kind as a special offering to the Lord.

> All those who owned the following items
> willingly brought them:
> blue, purple, and scarlet thread; fine linen and goat hair for cloth;
> and tanned ram skins and fine goatskin leather. And all who had
> silver and bronze objects gave them as a sacred offering to the
> Lord. And those who had acacia wood brought it for use in the
> project.

> All the women who were skilled in sewing
> and spinning prepared blue, purple, and scarlet thread,
> and fine linen cloth.
> All the women who were willing
> used their skills to spin the goat hair into yarn.

The leaders brought onyx stones and the special gemstones to be
set in the ephod and the priest's chestpiece. They also brought
spices and olive oil for the light, the anointing oil, and the fragrant
incense.

So the people of Israel—every man and woman who was eager
to help in the work the Lord had given them through Moses—
brought their gifts and gave them freely to the Lord.

(Exodus 34:20-29, NLT)

God was not looking for a place
that was built on fear.
There are no taxes,
forced tribute,
or demands on the people.

There is the call for a willing heart.
This is about making a different choice than Adam made.
It's about choosing to love God,
and give riches out of gratitude
for freedom
and blessings.
Out of the abundance of the heart,
out of what was inside,
the people gave.

Suddenly,
there is an army of artists and artisans,
and they have been given a commission,
to build a place for God.
And all this,
the riches of Egypt,
the raw materials and
luxury goods,
are all presented.

And for a second time in Scripture,
God calls the artist to lead.

THE CALL

One day my friend Alice was cracking an egg for breakfast.

There were two yolks.

The next day Alice made eggs again.

Two yolks, again.

And the third time it happened,
on the third day,
she paid attention.

And she went to her counselor and asked him about it.

He was very wise and said:
"Whenever God repeats something,
He is trying to get your attention."

I mentioned in an earlier chapter,
the lack of curiosity about Bezalel among scholars and leaders.

But there is a lot about Bezalel
that demands our attention.

Bezalel was called by God twice.

To my knowledge,
he is the only person in the Bible who has received two identical calls.

The first call came while Moses was on the mountain.
When God tells Moses
about the first call of Bezalel,
it is in the past tense.
God says to Moses,
"see I have called Bezalel by name
and I have filled him with my Spirit."

While the religious authorities
were creating a new religion around a golden calf
something was happening that was very important.

Somewhere in the midst of the camp,
Bezalel was having an experience with the Holy Spirit.
Some of my friends would say he was getting a "download" from heaven.
Bezalel received his call from God,
before
Moses heard about it.

Bezalel received revelation in the first calling
of all that God was telling Moses.

It was a private call.
And every call from God is at first hidden,
and private.
And Bezalel,
who carried a call for true worship,
to establish a place for God in the earth,
had to stand by and watch those
who were
not called
make idols.
Every call from God requires hiddenness,
testing,
and pain.

You get to watch
less called, and less gifted people
do your job,
and often do it better than you.

Every call from God sends you into the desert.
This is not a bug,
but a feature.
The one who calls
is determined
to teach you to trust the Voice.
You can only do this alone,
apart,
and sifted.
So that all the other props in your life are removed,
and all you have is the call of God.
And when everything is gone
but the memory
of the voice,
the encounter,
the angel,
or the vision,
you have to choose.

When all your human motivations,
and efforts are removed,
You have to make the choice.
Will you keep walking?

And you know you have to keep walking,
and follow the call from God.

And Bezalel illustrates an essential part of the process.
Public recognition.

There was the second call,
the public one.

Because,
after the call has been tested,
it needs to be affirmed and blessed—
in public.
The public recognition,
supplies legitimacy.
And Moses the father, acknowledges Bezalel, the son.

Exodus 35:30 says:
"See the Lord has called
by name
Bezalel,
son of Uri, son of Hur,
and filled him with the Spirit of God."

God called Bezalel
by name.

Twice.

Pay attention.

When God speaks,
something is created.

The Word of God is the sound of creativity.
And in Exodus,
the same word that is used to describe God
creating at the Creation,
is the word used for Bezalel's call.

A call from God is an act of creation.
Every prophetic word spoken is pregnant with possibility.
And every word from God is full of provision.
Because when God speaks,
something new is created.
And so the sound of the Word of God
is the sound of possibility.

It is the sound of abundance
and the sound of opportunity.

And it is no wonder
that this second call of Bezalel
comes within the context of the offering.

Because, after the private sifting,
Bezalel still has to affirm this word.
He has to respond to the call,
in a mighty public way.
And Bezalel responds to his call
in the midst of the offering of the heart.
And he is put in charge of all the skilful.
He too is an offering,
because when you hear the voice,
you must respond,
"Let it be to me according to your word."

In the call and response,
something is birthed and released.

The call of God contains an infinite supply.
The call of God contains all that is necessary.

And in the call
Bezalel is presented with
all the riches of Egypt,
and all the skilled who offer their abilities.

The call is a public endorsement of who he is
and what he is called to do.

Jesus called Peter,
James,
and John
and told them to leave their visible source of supply,
their nets,

the tools of their livelihood.
He told them to leave behind the things
that paid the bills,
that fed their families,
and defined their place in society.

They heard a voice,
and somewhere deep in their DNA,
they recognized the sound
that called the moon and the stars to shine.
Somewhere they recognized the voice of the One
who can call something out of nothing.

They went from the seen to the unseen,
and they left all that they knew.

And in exchange they received
12 baskets of leftover bread and fish.
They received houses and lands,
trips to Rome and the far ends of the earth,
Freedom from prisons,
and an everlasting name.

The voice that called creation,
and called Bezalel,
is the voice that calls you and me.

And within every call from God,
is the promise of provision,
and overwhelming possibility.

Doing things
from your own sense
of internal purpose
or your own deep personal convictions
is never enough.

You need the voice of the Father
calling you.

It is that self-creating sound
that makes everything possible.

During the first few years of my decision
to start Belonging House
there were a lot of challenges.

One day,
after observing another wave of problems and
difficulties,
a close friend remarked:

"You must have a call from God,
because anybody else would have
quit by now."

Let me tell you a rule of the universe:
the more clear the call,
the more severe the challenges.
The call is the Source of your authority.

If you know
that you know
that you know
God told you to do something,
then there will be no stopping you.
You have heard the creating voice of the Father.
And behind that voice is all the verve of heaven saying:
This is the way, walk in it.

The Voice gives direction.
The Voice gives authority,
and the Voice gives confidence,
to walk across any difficulty
and get to the other side.

Every kingdom artist
needs to hear the call
and know the creating voice of the Father.
If you are reading this book,
I am guessing that you are called.

Maybe you heard the Voice in the middle of the night.
And in quietness
and suffering,
the call has been tested.

> My child,
> when you come to serve the Lord,
> prepare yourself for testing.
> Set your heart right and be steadfast,
> and do not be impetuous in time of calamity.
> Cling to him and do not depart,
> so that your last days may be prosperous.
> Accept whatever befalls you,
> and in times of humiliation be patient.
> For gold is tested in the fire,
> and those found acceptable, in the furnace of humiliation.
> Trust in him, and he will help you;
> make your ways straight, and hope in him.
>   (Ecclesiasticus 2:1-6)

The Call of God makes everything possible.

There is more
than you can ever imagine.

Let me pray for you.

Father,
I thank you for the one who reads this,
who has heard your call
to become a warrior in your army of artists.
For those who have struggled,
who have been tested,
and who seem to go forward one step,
and back again two,
I pray for a sturdiness
to do the work at hand.
I pray that all the resources of heaven
would respond to your voice,
and they would experience
everything confirming their faith,
and they would receive the endorsement of heaven.

And for those,
who have not heard your call,
may their ears be opened
and their eyes see,
all that you have for those
who are called to build your place in the earth.

Release a mighty Kingdom revolution,
and cast the fear of the unknown
out of our lives.

Jesus you became the Image of the invisible God,
and we pray this prayer in your name.
Amen.

TENT OF THE FATHER

When God calls you,
you cannot do it alone.

Every real call from God is an impossible job.
And every impossible job from God
is going to demand skills that are beyond your gift set.

The two calls of Bezalel have three things in common:
an emphasis on the filling of the Holy Spirit,
a listing of supernatural abilities,
and the appointment of Oholiab, of the tribe of Dan.

Part of the calling of Bezalel
is the calling of his assistant.

And for the record,
the calling is never to "Bezalel and Oholiab."

The calling is to Bezalel,
they are not referred to as a team.
Scholars and commentators
generally lump them together,
and never explore the relationship.

Before we look at their relationship,
let's talk about Oholiab.

Oholiab is from the lowest tribe, the tribe of Dan.
His father, Ahisamach,
has a name that means
"my brother is my support,"
or "Close like a brother."

And Oholiab's name
is pretty straightforward:
"Tent of the Father."

Remember what I said about a name in the Bible?
A name often talks about
who a person is,
and what they are supposed to do.
It's all about identity.

And in the second list of giftings in Exodus 35,
the skills Oholiab receives
are specifically related to textiles:
embroiderer,
working in dyes and colors,
skill with fine linen,
weaving,
and design ability.

Like Bezalel,
Tent of the Father
is going to create the Father's Tent.

Jewish commentators,
more in tune to the nuances
of the original text,
are really very clear:
Bezalel is the Master
and he has received many assistants from the skilful.

And Moses
highlights one of these assistants by name to make a point.

Bezalel is from the highest tribe: Judah.
Oholiab is from the lowest,
because God lifts up the lowly,
and puts them with the princes of his people.
He takes a tent,
a lowly dwelling place,
and fills it with his presence.

Oholiab is the embodiment of the project,
just as Bezalel is the incarnation of the Artisan.
God's greatest resource is people,
and God gave Bezalel Oholiab as a core resource.

And out of the
continuous filling of the Holy Spirit
that is ongoing,
overflowing,
empowering,
and inspiring;
Oholiab is empowered.

Oholiab,
through his relationship
with Bezalel
receives a New Covenant
experience.

He experiences
supernatural grace,
and ability,
to become
a Tent of the Father,
the dwelling place of God,
a Tabernacle.

Because he comes under Bezalel's authority,
he receives all the blessings
of Bezalel.

God has lifted up the lowly,
and filled the hungry with good things.

And so, rather than
"Bezalel and Oholiab" as two throwaway characters at the end of Exodus,
we have
Bezalel the Master Artisan, and
Oholiab and all the Skilful.
Bezalel is an Image of Jesus,
the truest expression of the Image of God.
Oholiab is an image of the Church,
the tabernacle and dwelling place of the Holy Spirit.

And right from the call the work begins.

Meanwhile,
there has been an offering happening.

As I said,
the call of God contains
its own provision.
Some of that provision is people,
some of it is property,
and a lot of it is Presence.

So the Holy Spirit
filled Bezalel,
overflowed into Oholiab,
and stirred the hearts of all the skilful,
and all those who
had abundance to share.

Bezalel is the only artist
in history,

who asked his patrons
to stop giving.

> So Moses summoned Bezalel and Oholiab and all the others who
> were specially gifted by the Lord and were eager to get to work.
> Moses gave them the materials donated by the people of Israel
> as sacred offerings for the completion of the sanctuary. But the
> people continued to bring additional gifts each morning. Finally
> the craftsmen who were working on the sanctuary left their work.
> They went to Moses and reported, "The people have given more than
> enough materials to complete the job the Lord has commanded us
> to do!"
> So Moses gave the command, and this message was sent throughout
> the camp: "Men and women, don't prepare any more gifts for the
> sanctuary. We have enough!" So the people stopped bringing their
> sacred offerings. Their contributions were more than enough to
> complete the whole project. (Exodus 26:2-7, NLT)

Do you see a progression?

Identity leads to calling,
and calling leads to empowering,
and empowering leads to gifting,
and gifting leads to abundance.

Abundance
leads to generosity,
and then there is more than enough
for you
and for the kingdom.

Abundance
produces more work to do.
God calls you,
and gives you gifts,
not for you,
but for others
and the fulfillment of the plan.

God always gives us resources for the work.

There is always enough
at the Father's table.

When you lean into the call,
all the resources of heaven are attracted to you,
and God will provide
the people,
the provision,
and the Presence to make it happen.

A HOLY PLACE

Work is a beautiful thing.

It begins with the second call
and the offering,
and then the work
becomes a natural expression of the offering.

Up to this point,
this is a story about love.
About retaking
a renegade creation
as people make an act of will
to give from the heart.
And the skilful choose
to offer their abilities
in the service of God
and under the leadership of Bezalel.

And then,
things begin to build from lowly curtain rings
and curtains,
to pillars,
and then the ark of the Covenant.

Throughout,
there is a reference to an unknown "he."
Somewhere between Exodus 36:9 and 10,
the initial naming of "he" disappeared.
There is a problem in the text,
and we don't know who he is until Exodus 37:1
when "he" is identified.

Bezalel made the ark of the Covenant.

There is an element of abundance and overflowing through these three
chapters,
as work commences,
and it overflows out of the indwelling Holy Spirit.
It's a poem about work,
and a song about craftsmanship.
The process is as much worship,
as the liturgies
for which these
objects will be used.

We are coming to the climax of the Bezalel story.

God was looking for a place
to use as his "beachhead" on earth.
And the most important part,
the embassy of heaven
containing a model of the throne room in heaven,
was about to be completed.

Bezalel
took fragrant
acacia wood,
and made a chest
one and half cubits,
by two and half cubits.
And then he lined it all with gold leaf.

And then he made feet for the chest.
and to the feet,
at the ends of the chest,
he made rings of gold.

And he made a cover,
that would be called a "Mercy Seat."
And he made two cherubim,
with the heads of men,
the bodies of lions,
and the wings of eagles,
and placed them
eyes down,
on either end of the mercy seat.

The wings bent forward,
to indicate the place where the glory would abide.

At the ends of the chest,
he inserted poles.
Not across the front as is typically
shown in pictures,
but at the ends.
This unstable design forced the bearers of the Ark
to face one another
and to bow,
and to walk slow.

By design
they could not turn away from the Presence,
and they became a living
enactment of the throne in heaven
where four living creatures
continually cry
Holy,
Holy,
Holy.

And this chest,
the Ark of the Covenant,
would lead the People to the Promised Land.
It would lead them across the Jordan River,
it would lead them around the walls of Jericho,
and it would lead them into battle.

Bezalel made a throne for God in the earth.
A place for the glory to rest.
He made a throne room
with a lampstand,
and a place for the bread of the Presence.
He made an altar,
and he made the incense and the anointing oil.

Then Bezalel made an altar,
and he made a courtyard.

It is all a beautiful sacrifice
of work
and worship
to make a place to get close to God.
That's the point, remember,
for God,
the Most Relational Being in the Universe,
to get close to
his Little Creators.
This was not designed
to be a place
where people come to pay their
sin tax.

No, in Hebrew
the word for sacrifice
is rooted in the word for "close."
The nearest word in Hebrew to Sacrifice
is
Family.

I mentioned this earlier,
but it bears repeating.

You make sacrifices
to become close
and in doing this,
you become a family.

God is building a portable
palace
with a throne room,
a throne,
and a banqueting hall
so the people he loves
can be close.
He is giving them a place to belong in the earth,
Regardless of their wanderings.
So they can eat and drink in his presence.
And all the nations of the earth can see
that God has done wonders for Israel.

And all of this had a maker.
Bezalel gets credit.
And he is leading a team,
although they are not mentioned.
You know that Oholiab
has blue and purple hands.
And there are armies of women,
former master weavers in Egypt
making fine linen garments,
giggling,
and gossiping,
and singing,
as they do the work.
And there is the sound of foundries,
and the sound of hammer upon metal.
There is the smell of sawdust,
and scent of incense.

There are the groans of men carrying poles,
and the sounds of lectures
as Bezalel and Oholiab
teach how to care for and maintain
these objects when they travel.

And then,
It seems this story ends abruptly.

Bezalel is never honored,
or thanked,
or acknowledged again,
after the description of this work.
There is a sudden interruption in the narrative.

We never see Bezalel present his work to Moses.
We never hear of Bezalel saying goodbye to the Ark.
And we never hear about a final
blessing upon Bezalel and the leaders.

When you do a job for God
it is the Presence
in the midst of the work
that needs to satisfy.

Because,
as we shall see in the next chapter,
for the artist and creator,
human praise is
unreliable.

Written right into the Bible,
is the eternal struggle between "the system"
and the Spirit;
between the creative person,
and the authorities.

The Hebrew mind often
puts two seemingly conflicting ideas
side by side.

Truth is found in the tension
of pondering and processing.

TRUTH IN TENSION

When you get a really good look at parts of the Bible,
and you spend time with them,
you start to find surprises.

Nothing really should be surprising
in a book that is four thousand years old.
Even if one person wrote all of it,
after four thousand years,
a lot of people would have touched it.

Some people make the Bible say things
the Bible never says about itself.
And sometimes people lose their faith
because of rigid claims that do not hold up
under closer inspection.

I was not raised in church.
When I went to a Christian College,
I made a shocking discovery.
Many of my classmates lost their faith
when the rigid things they believed were challenged.
Their churches told them to stop thinking,
and to believe some things about the Bible
that could not stand up to scrutiny.

They were taught to put their brains in storage
if they wanted to be Christians.
It's unfortunate, because
you need to think if you are going to make a difference.

Let's be clear.

The Bible says that it is inspired by God
and it contains everything we need
for teaching,
training,
and salvation. (II Timothy 3:16-17)

The Bible says that the Word of our God shall stand forever, (Isaiah 40:8)
and that it is living and active,
dividing soul and spirit. (Hebrews 4:12)

And Jesus said "you search the scriptures
thinking that in them you will find life,
but the scriptures point to me,
and I am the source of life." (John 5:39)

Jesus also said we cannot edit out the things in the Bible
we may not like or disagree with. (Matthew 5:18-19)

The Bible has authority,
contains the power to change lives,
and is the guide for how we need to live.
The Bible provides the source of our faith,
and is also the direction for how we are to live.
The Bible is all about Jesus,
the living embodiment of the Word.
The Bible does not claim to be without textual error.
Even though there are no errors regarding Truth.
The Bible does not claim to be infallible,
even though it does claim inspiration.
The Bible, unlike the Qur'an or the Book of Mormon,
doesn't claim to have dropped out of heaven

or to be the words of one particular prophet.
The Bible doesn't even say who is allowed to interpret it.
And for our discussion,
the Bible does not claim that Moses wrote the first five books.
And that one is very important,
because the traditions of men say Moses did.

The Jewish community has a sense of organic connection
to the Scriptures, and how we received them.
A Jewish person sees themselves in the pages of the Bible.
Because of this,
the Jewish community is
somewhat comfortable with the fact
that during the Babylonian captivity,
when there was nothing else to do,
Levites and Scribes
to pass the time,
took all the old scrolls and parchments
and the familiar stories
passed down for hundreds of years,
and compiled the Old Testament.

There were many hands involved,
and there was probably
discussion,
polishing,
disagreement,
and editing.
And I imagine, just like Bible translation today,
some decisions were made in committee.

And about three hundred years later,
the Hebrew was translated into Greek.
That Greek version is what Jesus and the Apostles
quote in the New Testament.
We know they used a committee of seventy to make that version.

Inspiration is an amazing thing.

The Holy Spirit
is involved in the
writing,
editing,
translating,
interpreting,
printing,
and distributing
of the Bible.
It is a miracle,
because when you compare the thousands of manuscripts,
the problems and differences are minor.
There is nothing else like it in ancient literature
in terms of numbers of copies,
and level of agreement.

And those scribes in Babylon
believed that what they were doing was important
because the nation
was nearly destroyed,
and although they disregarded
the covenant in freedom,
the covenant became important
in captivity.

The Scriptures
had become their greatest treasure.
They are still a treasure to Jews today,
so much so, that you cannot even throw away a worn out scroll.

And there is something else we need to remember.

Context is everything,
and these Scribes and Levites
were men of their time.

In the ancient world
blacksmiths and people who could make idols
were worshipped.

It seems logical, if you can make a god,
you are probably more powerful than the god you made.
Many scholars note,
that Bezalel
is the only person in the entire Old Testament
who is given the attributes
of a god.

He is a Creator,
Filled with the Holy Spirit,
able to empower others,
he receives tribute,
and his physical activity is described in detail.
He seems to create out of nothing.
His three chapters of work in Exodus
are pretty unique when you consider it is a book about Moses.

And so,
out of nowhere
it seems the Bezalel story is interrupted.

Bezalel's story doesn't end.
Instead, the style and tone of the story changes.

> These are the records of the tabernacle, the tabernacle of the
> covenant, which were drawn up at the commandment of Moses,
> the work of the Levites being under the direction of Ithamar son
> of the priest Aaron. Bezalel son of Uri son of Hur, of the tribe of
> Judah, made all that the Lord commanded Moses; and with him was
> Oholiab son of Ahisamach, of the tribe of Dan, engraver, designer,
> and embroiderer in blue, purple, and crimson yarns, and in fine linen.
> (Exodus 38:21-23)

Suddenly there is a different record of the Tabernacle.
The literary style changes, and the descriptions of work that Bezalel was
doing is not completed.

There are a few more things to point out.

In this record,
Moses is the initiator,
not God.
The Tabernacle is now
not the work of all the people,
but the work of the Levites.
Moses draws up the plans,
and he puts a Levite,
Ithamar the son of Aaron, in charge.
Ithamar is an administrator,
and it's not clear if Moses initiated the plans or this record.
As a gentle reminder,
Ithamar was not mentioned by God on the mountain.

There is a brief
reference to Bezalel and Oholiab.
There are no details about their gifts
and no mention of the Holy Spirit.
Although it is noted they are artists, designers,
engravers, and embroiderers.

And further on it says the Tabernacle was built not with offerings
but with a temple tax.
And the tax was initiated
and overseen
by the Levites.

We went from an offering of the heart
moved by the Holy Spirit,
where the supply exceeded the need,
to tribute commanded by the Levites,
and a census.

And this is a very important detail,
they are required to pay the tax
using coins
from the time of Solomon's Temple.

And then
for the next two chapters
the phrase "As the Lord commanded Moses"
is repeated 19 times.
And Moses
rather than Bezalel
installs all the elements of the Tabernacle.
Moses is superhuman,
in this retelling.
Or maybe SuperLevite.
He hangs all the curtains,
puts all the things in place,
moves all the furniture,
and does all the installation.

19 is the number representing "perfect judgement" in Jewish thought.

The emphasis in this version
is on the robes,
insignia,
and offices of the priests.
And in the end,
Moses blesses all Israel,
but never mentions
Bezalel
and Oholiab.

So before the story of Bezalel is over,
the main characters
are written out.
It takes a careful eye
to recognize
that someone later on,
a Levite,
and a member of the unemployed Temple priesthood,
has made some revisions
to make sure Moses is still the boss.

This Levite's temple has been destroyed,
and his reason for being is in danger.
And in Babylon
there are spirit led prophets like Ezekiel running around
telling people what to do.
Someone has to make sure that order is maintained.

You can imagine the thought process.

How could Moses not be filled with the Holy Spirit,
when these artists were?
And how can the Bible contain high praises for
people who are the very embodiment of idolatry?
It was Moses who led the nation, and established the Law.

How could the Tabernacle be built by outsiders
when the Levites were in charge of worship?

And so
in the end,
Bezalel made some beautiful objects.
The Menorah and the Ark have filled our imaginations
for centuries.
But Moses has received all the credit.

You may not agree with me,
but this thought process
continued later into the Talmud.

Rabbis made it clear
that Moses did the building
and Bezalel was a thirteen year old boy
(he needed to be Bar Mitzvahed, of course)
and Moses manipulated his hands from behind
like a puppet.

My theological education spanned eight years.
When I was in seminary there was only one sentence
about building the Tabernacle.

The professor said,
"Moses did it. You can read about it when you have time."
Judging from the letters I get from pastors,
I doubt anybody had time.

In Deuteronomy 10:3
at the end of his life,
Moses retold the story as well.

> So I made an ark of acacia wood, cut two tablets of stone like the
> former ones, and went up the mountain with the two tablets in my
> hand. So I turned and came down from the mountain, and put the
> tablets in the ark that I had made; and there they are, as the Lord
> commanded me.

Yes, this is a clear contradiction of Exodus 37:1.
Moses took credit for the ark,
and not just in a "the artists worked under Moses' direction" way,
but he said he actually did it.

The Bible is "a warts and all" kind of book.

Later on
in II Chronicles,
Bezalel is mentioned
as the maker of the bronze altar.
He gets mentioned there because all the kings are
from the tribe of Judah,
like Bezalel.

Chronicles is a retelling of the history of Israel
from the perspective of the kings and the prophets.

What's going on here?

First,
we have two rival tribes, Levi and Judah.

Levi was given the job of running the religious system of Israel.
Judah was given the promise
of ruling the nation,
and one day producing
the king who would rule forever.

Throughout scripture,
beginning here with Bezalel,
there is tension.

Bezalel is a charismatic leader.
His authority didn't come from Moses,
but from God.
He is given authority over all the skilled workers,
and has supernatural ability to teach and lead.

Aaron, on the other hand,
although chosen by God to lead,
has the legacy of building a golden calf,
and has his authority questioned throughout his life.

Moses doesn't get to enter the Promised Land.
There is something about the character of Moses,
and the leadership of Aaron,
that is tested throughout the books of the Torah.

Like leaders throughout history,
insecurity
is a constant companion.

The Bible contains these conflicts and contradictions.
Just like there is a tension between idolatry and art,
there is a tension between artists and leaders.
And it's here,
right in the text.

And the tension between these two tribes,
and the leaders

and the talented,
will continue.

It's in the New Testament.
A group of Levites will go to the Romans
and demand
that an upstart preacher
from the tribe of Judah named Jesus
be crucified.
It will be the Levites
who demand that the sign
"Jesus of Nazareth, King of the Jews"
be removed.

A group of Levites will stone Stephen,
and imprison Peter and John because
"He spoke against Moses,
and the traditions of the Temple."

There is always a tension between God's Plan
and the religious system.
And it echoes right down to today.

We are given two different perspectives on how the Tabernacle was built.

The Holy Spirit calls, fills and empowers
an artist named Image of God,
and then moves everyone to give
out of the abundance of their heart.
The artist leads a team and they create a Tabernacle
matching Moses'
revelation on the mountain.

and

Moses draws up plans
his nephew is put in charge to execute them
and the nephew hires two artists.

The people are taxed to pay for the project,
and Moses does the final installation and takes the credit.

Yes, the Bible does contradict itself.
Your God is bigger than you have been told.
He is big enough to allow contrary opinions
in the Bible He inspired.
Your God is big enough to be secure in the face of human insecurities.

Somewhere,
in the tension
is the truth.

And here we have the tension between
the religious spirit
and the Holy Spirit.

The religious spirit
is concerned with should, ought, and try harder.
It works from the outside in.
It always asks the question:
"By what authority
do you do these things?"
It is man centered.
It makes sure you follow the rules,
and do things decently and in order.
It makes plans,
based on human designs,
and then asks God to bless them.
It puts demands on people,
and makes sure you pay your taxes to God.
And it uses
guilt,
fear,
and manipulation
to keep people in their place.

On the other hand,
the Holy Spirit
works from the inside out.
He calls the outsider,
even before the leader knows about it.
The Holy Spirit
puts a law in your heart,
and the desire to please God.
He works in process over procedure,
and brings order out of chaos.
The Holy Spirit can put the plan in more than one person
and trusts them all to carry it out.
He says "whoever is not against me is for me" and
knows there are sheep not of this fold who have heard the Shepherds voice.

The plan is a new humanity,
a community that represents heaven,
and people in fellowship with God and one another.
And people are messy.

Not surprisingly,
these two systems often collide.
And somehow,
this glorious,
truthful,
divinely inspired Book
has allowed us to see it.

Your God is so big
that He has sown the seeds of insurrection
within the pages of His Bible.
He has always wanted to undermine
the idolatry of the religious professional.
And this is why we need to be constantly reforming
against the traditions of men.

The fact that the Bible says Bezalel made the Ark
and Moses later claimed to make it

shouldn't shake your faith.
It should make us have a deeper understanding
about why Moses
didn't go into the Promised Land.
Sometimes a great leader
cannot lead you into the new thing God really wants to do.
God uses broken people.
God knows that leaders have limitations,
and He is limitless supply.
As I mentioned,
right from the beginning,
there was a plan,
and that plan was to establish the Kingdom of God
on the earth.

And over time
that plan was obscured by the failures
and fancies of Israel.
And some of the responsibility for failure
falls on the Levites.
It's all in the Bible for us to see.
They didn't teach,
lead,
or maintain
the Tabernacle built by Bezalel.

And yet,
the Kingdom is always advancing,
never retreating.
God is still taking territory.

Maybe you have been crushed by a leader or a church.
Maybe you have been erased from the last chapter of the story,
after all the hard work and energy has been spent.
Bezalel is the pattern and prototype for every kingdom artist.

So many of the people I coach and for whom I pray
have been hurt.

Good people do bad things when their authority is threatened.
And prophetic people are messy.
When God gets hold of a life,
it often directly challenges the religious order.
It is hard to have authority
and control
when God keeps
talking to people
without consulting you.

I have lived on both sides of this divide,
within the religious establishment
and outside on a wild adventure
with the Holy Spirit.

There is a tension
between structure
and freedom.

Don't be afraid to think.

Walk toward the tension
and the seeming contradictions,
and ask the Holy Spirit
to teach you.

I'm sorry if you have been hurt or overlooked by a leader.
I'm sorry if someone misquoted the Bible
and said artists should work for free.
I'm sorry if someone took credit for your hard work.
I'm sorry if a leader rewarded someone else over you,
because they thought another one "could be trusted."
I'm sorry if you were not paid when you had an agreement.
I'm sorry if you were used,
and I am sorry if you were abused.

This wasn't a new humanity or the Kingdom.

On behalf of the leaders and the church,
please forgive me.

Some of you run from churches and authority,
and you need them.
Some of you are living in isolation
and living lives of rebellion.

Come back,
get close,
and rejoin the community.

We need you,
and you need us.

Somewhere in the tension
is the Truth.

LITTLE CREATOR

I once was going to join a monastery,
and they taught me about contemplation.
Contemplation is the art of meditating on
and pondering the mysteries of God as a form of prayer.

Some concepts you can contemplate for hours
and never reach the end.
There is always more.

You can contemplate the Cross forever.
You can ponder the words of Jesus forever.
And you can meditate on Mary's encounter with Gabriel forever.
And now I have learned,
after 10 years of
contemplation,
study,
and prayer,
that Bezalel is a source of endless contemplation.
And in each go round,
God gets bigger, and more glorious.

There is no one else like Bezalel in the Old Testament.
He's the only character in the Bible
who has been actively suppressed throughout history.

As I mentioned,
scholars note that
Bezalel is described in ways
only reserved for God.

In one of the books I wrote about Bezalel,
I said he might be a Christophany
that is, an Old Testament appearance of Jesus.
And there is a strong case for that.
Bezalel is of the tribe of Judah,
he is filled with the Holy Spirit,
he has disciples he teaches, and to whom he imparts the Holy Spirit.
He receives his source of supplies from the Passover,
and sacrifices his greatest work
and never sees it again
after it goes into the Holy of Holies.

He is a mysterious person,
and we don't know where he went after
the Tabernacle was complete.

I have guessed he may have had a hand in making the Brazen Serpent.
He has all the gifts and abilities to do so.
Again, Moses gets credit for making the Serpent,
so we will never know for sure.

Bezalel crackles with mystery,
and with eternity.

Melchizedek was called a Christophany in Hebrews,
with only three similarities to Jesus.
Bezalel has about twelve parallels to Jesus.

But, for you and me it means nothing
if he is an example of the pre-Incarnate Christ.
That's just a scholarly theory that has nothing to do with us.
But it means something if we can be like Bezalel.

Bezalel was filled with the Spirit of God,
and was given skill
and was given a team
and was given resources.
The Holy Spirit made him like Jesus.

When God calls you,
your calling is to be a Little Creator.
Not only are you made in the image and likeness of God,
you are created to be a new creation.
A transformed humanity,
living from the inside out.

God made you to be a tabernacle and an ark.
You were intended to be the Temple of the Holy Spirit.
You were created to house the glory,
and become a little replica of heaven.
And in doing this,
you too can be the person
who is most like Jesus in the world around you.

In John 14 Jesus said he was going away,
to prepare a place for us.

At the end of the Book,
the place that Jesus is working on
descends out of heaven.

> So he took me in the Spirit to a great, high mountain, and he showed me the holy city, Jerusalem, descending out of heaven from God. It shone with the glory of God and sparkled like a precious stone—like jasper as clear as crystal. The city wall was broad and high, with twelve gates guarded by twelve angels. And the names of the twelve tribes of Israel were written on the gates. There were three gates on each side—east, north, south, and west. The wall of the city had twelve foundation stones, and on them were written the names of the twelve apostles of the Lamb. (Revelation 21:10-14, NLT)

A few years ago
I noted that the first gifts given to Bezalel—
the ability to work in precious metals and gold
and the ability to engrave names on gemstones
—correlated with the description of the city.

God is the Artist and Designer.
God is the Master Artisan,
and the source of all our creativity.
Somehow Jesus is closely aligned with Bezalel.
And he is continuing to create in us
a city not made with hands.

The Author of Beauty
can make you beautiful
from the inside out.
The same Spirit
that released a seventeen-fold gifting
into Bezalel
can empower you.

And you can be more than just gifted
and talented.
You can be more than successful and prosperous.
You can make beautiful things,
and be a beautiful thing.

Imagine a community of artists and artisans,
who are shaping culture,
without the
competition,
cattiness,
and drama
we associate with the arts.

Being like Jesus
and like Bezalel
is possible.

The Holy Spirit from the inside out
can transform your loves,
and reform your desires.
And you can be a work of art
and reflect the assignment God
ordained for you
before time began.

Not only can you make incredible products that will change the world,
you can be a product of grace,
and bear fruit.
Love,
joy,
peace,
patience,
kindness,
gentleness,
self-control,
generosity,
and faithfulness.

They go hand in hand—
being creative,
and being holy.

"For we are God's masterpiece.
He has created us anew in Christ Jesus,
so we can do the good things he planned for us long ago."
(Ephesians 2:10, NLT)

"For God knew us and called us,
and chose us to be little icons of his Son."
(Romans 8:29, author's translation)

This may be the greatest mystery of all
to be an artist who is also a work of art.
Allowing the heat and hammering
of the Lord

to transform you
as a reflection of his glory,
the seat of his presence,
a sacrifice of praise,
and a member of his family.

It's all about identity,
knowing who you are.
You are a Little Creator,
you are the Image of God.

Are you confident in the bigness of God?
Are you able to rest in the knowledge
that you are blessed,
and called,
and empowered?
May you be a Bezalel,
the Image of God in the earth.
The whole earth is groaning
for the revealing of the sons and daughters of God.
Come forth Little Creator,
walk into your true image
and breathe in the breath of life.
Let the Holy Spirit
come in and take control,
take territory in your heart,
and take territory in the earth.
It is all part of the plan
to make this renegade creation
an outpost of heaven.

VISIBLE IMAGE

This book began with a Greek word.

Icon.

And many times,
Paul and the New Testament,
point to Jesus,
and they call him the "Icon."
Sadly, in most cases
translators uses any phrase to avoid
what the Greek says:
like same substance,
co-equal, and
consubstantial.
In the Bible, in Greek,
it says icon.

And then we stumble upon this passage in 2 Corinthians.
> Now the Lord is the Spirit,
> and where the Spirit of the Lord is, there is freedom.
> And all of us, with unveiled faces,
> seeing the glory of the Lord as though reflected in a mirror,
> are being transformed into the same image
> from one degree of glory to another;
> for this comes from the Lord, the Spirit. (II Corinthians 3:17-18)

Jesus
is the Icon.
And if we are filled and overflowing
like Bezalel,
we begin to be etched and transformed,
as a work of art.
And when we look in the mirror,
Paul says
we should see the Icon.
We should see Jesus,
because the Holy Spirit
has removed
all the layers of paint,
and dust,
and sin,
and brokenness,
and we have become a True Image.
Living Icons, of the Master Icon.
We have discovered our True Identity,
and become bearers of glory,
just like in the beginning.

> The Father is looking for a Bride for His Son,
> who will join together in a Royal Wedding,
> and inherit a Kingdom.

Like Bezalel who
created a place for Israel
to prepare for the coming of the Lord,
God is looking
for Little Creators,
reflections of his Icon,
to once again,
make an outpost of heaven,
and prepare the way for the Coming of the Lord.

God is looking for creative and unconventional people
who are disciples of Jesus.

Bona fide New Testament Christians
who deliver the Kingdom where ever they go.
A company who can say:

> The Spirit of the Sovereign Lord is upon me,
>   for the Lord has anointed me
>   to bring good news to the poor.
> He has sent me to comfort the brokenhearted
>   and to proclaim that captives will be released
>   and prisoners will be freed.
> He has sent me to tell those who mourn
>   that the time of the Lord's favor has come,
>   and with it, the day of God's anger against their enemies.
> To all who mourn in Israel,
>   he will give a crown of beauty for ashes,
> a joyous blessing instead of mourning,
>   festive praise instead of despair.
> In their righteousness, they will be like great oaks
>   that the Lord has planted for his own glory.
> They will rebuild the ancient ruins,
>   repairing cities destroyed long ago.
> They will revive them,
>   though they have been deserted for many generations.
>   (Isaiah 61:1-4, NLT)

I made a commitment
many years ago,
that I would say "yes" to everything,
listen to the Lord,
and do what He tells me.

My life became an adventure,
and we now have a company of men and women
who say like Mary,
"let it be to me according to your word."

> Maybe you have been content to be "a Christian artist"
> or a worldly artist who happens to call yourself a Christian.

I am extending my hand to you today,
and invite you to live for something greater,
to extend the rule and reign of the King and his Kingdom,
and to prepare the way for the Coming of the Lord.
Will you be a Visible Image of Jesus?

If so, join me in the commitment I have made.

I will believe on the Lord Jesus Christ, and love other people.
I will surrender myself to the Holy Spirit,
    and depend on his supernatural help.
I will attend to the Breaking of the Bread and Prayer.
I will stay in relationship with others who are passionate about Jesus.
I will saturate myself in all of the Bible and let its story become my story.
I will listen to the Lord, and do what He tells me.
I will pursue excellence in my craft,
    and continually choose to grow and learn.
I will go low, become a servant, and trust that God will raise me up.
I will become more aware of Christ in me, the hope of glory.
I will live a life of generosity.
I will embrace my vocation as an artist, artisan or creative professional,
    no matter my medium, knowing that God wants to transform
    the kingdoms of this world into the Kingdom of our Lord
    through the arts and creativity.
I will live a life of expectation knowing Christ will come again.

The world doesn't need
another Christian Artist.
Using the world's methods
to get their shallow products before the masses.
The world needs to see Jesus.

Are you willing
to offer yourself freely,
and be willing to let Jesus
be the one who is seen.
So that when someone looks at the good work
you have done,
they see Jesus.

Bezalel stepped back,
and became an Icon,
Secure in who he was.
You too can be a Bezalel.
The image of God.

O Author of Beauty,
who was first revealed as Creator,
when your Holy Spirit hovered over the waters;
and who filled Bezalel to build the Ark.
Raise up an Army of Artists in our day
who will build you a Throne in the earth,
and make a way for the Coming of the Lord.

Fill us,
renew us,
and make us bearers of your glory.
May your kingdom be established,
and your throne be extended
by the good work of our hands,
and the expressions of our creativity.
Through the Icon of the Invisible God,
Jesus Christ.
Amen.

For more information,
and to see the in depth research behind this book,
check out my earlier book:
Bezalel: Redeeming a Renegade Creation,
available at Amazon.com.

To find out more about the author,
go to christjohnotto.com.

To make the Belonging House Commitment, go to belonginghouse.org
You can also receive my Friday email, designed to encourage, challenge, and
transform.

Shalom.

ABOUT THE AUTHOR

Christ John Otto is the founder of Belonging House, a relational and spiritual fellowship of artists and creative people who are called to build Jesus a throne in the earth.

For more information,
please go to Belonginghouse.org